S. Hrg. 113–540

EVALUATING THE IMPACT OF THE "UMBRELLA MOVEMENT"

HEARING

BEFORE THE

SUBCOMMITTEE ON EAST ASIAN AND PACIFIC AFFAIRS

OF THE

COMMITTEE ON FOREIGN RELATIONS
UNITED STATES SENATE

ONE HUNDRED THIRTEENTH CONGRESS

SECOND SESSION

DECEMBER 3, 2014

Printed for the use of the Committee on Foreign Relations

Available via the World Wide Web: http://www.gpo.gov/fdsys/

U.S. GOVERNMENT PUBLISHING OFFICE

92–750 PDF   WASHINGTON : 2015

For sale by the Superintendent of Documents, U.S. Government Publishing Office
Internet: bookstore.gpo.gov   Phone: toll free (866) 512–1800; DC area (202) 512–1800
Fax: (202) 512–2104   Mail: Stop IDCC, Washington, DC 20402–0001

CONTENTS

ADDITIONAL MATERIAL SUBMITTED FOR THE RECORD

(III)

EVALUATING THE IMPACT OF THE "UMBRELLA MOVEMENT"

WEDNESDAY, DECEMBER 3, 2014

U.S. SENATE,
SUBCOMMITTEE ON EAST ASIAN AND PACIFIC AFFAIRS,
COMMITTEE ON FOREIGN RELATIONS,
Washington, DC.

The subcommittee met, pursuant to notice, at 9:30 a.m., in room SD–419, Dirksen Senate Office Building, Hon. Benjamin L. Cardin (chairman of the subcommittee) presiding.

Present: Senators Cardin and Rubio.

OPENING STATEMENT OF HON. BENJAMIN L. CARDIN, U.S. SENATOR FROM MARYLAND

Senator CARDIN. Let me welcome you all to the Subcommittee on East Asian and Pacific Affairs.

I have checked with Senator Rubio, and he consented that, because of the time issues—and that is that there are a series of votes that should take, unfortunately, the rest of the morning, starting at about 10 o'clock this morning and because of other scheduled meetings of the Senate Foreign Relations Committee, including a meeting with King Abdullah and a hearing on Iran sanctions, it is not possible to extend this hearing beyond the very short period of time that we have available.

So, I thank the witnesses for their understanding, and we are going to try to expedite this. There may be questions for the record, because we may not have time to ask all the questions. And I would ask the witnesses to please respond to questions that may be asked for the record that normally would have been given.

This will be the last hearing that I chair for the Subcommittee on East Asian and Pacific Affairs. And I really want to thank Senator Rubio for his help and cooperation. I think we have had a good schedule of hearings on the Rebalance to Asia and all the different components of it. We started with human rights, and we end with human rights.

And I thank Danny Russel, the Assistant Secretary, who has been incredibly helpful to us in understanding the issues, has worked very closely with our committee.

And, Danny, I thank you personally for all of your help.

I do want to acknowledge the staff that have been, I think, incredibly helpful to me. I had a lot of experience in Europe, not much in Asia, and they really covered for me well, and I want to thank them all personally for doing that. Algene Sarjery, of my staff, who has been incredibly helpful; Kelly Swaine, who is a detailee from the Department of State; Michael Schiffer, from the committee staff; Carolyn Leddy, Victor Cervino, and Jamie Fly, from Senator Rubio's staff. All of them have really made, I think, the work of this subcommittee very productive. It was certainly done in a nonpartisan way, and I thank them for their help.

We clearly have a very serious issue regarding what is going on in Hong Kong today. The last 48 hours have been very disturbing. We saw some violence, and we saw the end of this phase of the protests without the accomplishment of universal suffrage, which was a commitment given by the Chinese Government as a followup to the original Joint Declaration. So, clearly, we are concerned about that. There is legislation pending in the Congress to deal with this. The United States acted, in 1992, in the United States-Hong Kong Policy Act, saying human rights are of great importance to the United States and directly relevant to U.S. interests. And we gave Hong Kong status as a separate entity, but the President can take that status away if he believes Hong Kong is not sufficiently autonomous to justify such treatment.

So, Secretary Russel, it is a pleasure to have you here.

And, without objection, all of your written statements will be made part of the record, for both panels, and the members' opening statements will also be made part of the record.

Secretary Russel.

STATEMENT OF THE HON. DANIEL RUSSEL, ASSISTANT SECRETARY FOR EAST ASIAN AND PACIFIC AFFAIRS, U.S. DEPARTMENT OF STATE, WASHINGTON, DC

Mr. RUSSEL. Thank you very much, Mr. Chairman. And I thank you both for the opportunity to testify on this important and timely topic, but also thanks to you, personally, for your leadership and your partnership as chairman of this subcommittee.

Secretary Kerry has made the U.S. position very clear, in public and in private. An open society with a high degree of autonomy and rule of law has made Hong Kong successful and is essential to its future stability and prosperity. So, the United States supports universal suffrage and the aspirations of the Hong Kong people under the ''one country, two system'' framework.

As President Obama said at a press conference in Beijing last month with President Xi Jinping standing right next to him, the United States consistently speaks out on the right of people to express themselves and encourages that the elections in Hong Kong are transparent and fair and reflective of the opinions of the people there. We believe that the legitimacy of the Hong King Chief Executive will be greatly enhanced by universal suffrage, by an election that provides the people of Hong Kong a meaningful choice of candidates representative of the voters' will. This means allowing for a competitive election in which a range of candidates with different policy approaches are given an opportunity to seek the support of eligible Hong Kong voters.

In regard to the ongoing pro-democracy demonstrations in Hong Kong, the United States has consistently emphasized our support for freedom of assembly and freedom of expression, and we have encouraged both sides to address their differences peacefully through dialogue. And we have been clear, in the face of Chinese allegations, that the United States is not in any way involved in the protests. In fact, it is disingenuous to suggest that this debate is driven by outsiders, when it is so clearly about Hong Kongers' own hopes for their future.

It is important to note that the electoral reform process in Hong Kong is still underway. The debate is ongoing, and legislative action is planned for the first half of 2015. Failure to enact reforms would be a setback. We, therefore, encourage Beijing, the Hong Kong Government, and the people of Hong Kong to work together to ensure that a competitive process for the selection of the Chief Executive through universal suffrage is established for 2017. A multicandidate, competitive election would be a major step in Hong Kong's, and indeed the People's Republic of China's, political development.

The United States and Hong Kong are bound by shared values, economic and cultural relations, and people-to-people ties. Hong Kong has long protected fundamental freedoms. It is number one on the Heritage Foundation's Economic Freedom Index. It is the ninth-largest market for U.S. exports. It is a key source of foreign direct investment in the United States. That gives the United States, as well as China, a vested interest in preserving the system and autonomy of Hong Kong that brings stability and prosperity. That is why we stress the importance of China upholding its commitments. That is why we continue to speak out clearly and remain engaged on Hong Kong.

Thank you. I welcome your questions.

[The prepared statement of Mr. Russel follows:]

PREPARED STATEMENT OF DANIEL RUSSEL

INTRODUCTION

Today's hearing is timely given the debate taking place in Hong Kong over electoral reforms and the implementation of universal suffrage for the 2017 selection of Hong Kong's next Chief Executive. I welcome this opportunity to share with the committee the administration's views and response to political developments in Hong Kong, particularly with regard to the National People's Congress Standing Committee's (NPCSC) August 31 decision and the Hong Kong Government's response to the protests. I would also like to touch on the importance of our relationship with Hong Kong under the "One Country, Two Systems" framework.

Secretary Kerry is watching the situation in Hong Kong closely. The administration believes that an open society, with a high degree of autonomy and governed by the rule of law, is essential for Hong Kong's stability and prosperity—indeed this is what has made Hong Kong such a successful and truly global city. As we do around the world, the United States advocates in China for internationally recognized fundamental freedoms, such as freedom of peaceful assembly and freedom of expression.

Long before Hong Kong made its way into headlines, we made clear to Beijing our support for universal suffrage and the aspirations of the Hong Kong people under the "One Country, Two Systems" framework. We will not back off on that support. We have reaffirmed our position publicly and privately in numerous meetings with Chinese and Hong Kong officials at all levels of government. Most recently, Secretary Kerry raised Hong Kong in meetings with Chinese interlocutors in the runup to the APEC summit in Beijing, and President Obama made these points there in his meetings with President Xi. As the President said at a press conference in Beijing with President Xi standing next to him, the United States is going to "consistently speak out on the right of people to express themselves, and encourage that the elections that take place in Hong Kong are transparent and fair and reflective of the opinions of people there."

The "One Country, Two Systems" model, which is a long-standing Chinese position put forward by Deng Xiaoping and reflected in the PRC's Constitution, has provided a solid foundation for our strong relationship with Hong Kong. It means, among other things, that China accepts that Hong Kong government will retain its own legislative and judicial powers, as well as its own laws. And it means that Hong Kong's freedoms should be guaranteed by the PRC. At the time of reversion in 1997, China—under the "Basic Law"—committed to several important principles: "One Country, Two Systems," "Hong Kong people governing Hong Kong," maintenance of "a high degree of autonomy," and that the Chief Executive and all the members of the Legislative Council should be elected by "universal suffrage."

The "One Country, Two Systems" principle has enabled Hong Kong to flourish as an important example of prosperity, tolerance, open expression, and free market ideals. "One Country, Two Systems" has been central to Hong Kong's economic success. Hong Kong currently ranks first in the Heritage Foundation's Index of Economic Freedom. The PRC, I would note, ranks 137th.

Mr. Chairman, preserving Hong Kong's unique system and character serves the best interests of all parties. So we are concerned by signs that China's commitment to the "One Country, Two Systems" model, as well as to maintaining a high degree of autonomy, are eroding. While Hong Kong's media environment remains far less restricted than on the mainland, the steady downward trend in media freedom is troubling. The ability of Hong Kong's judiciary system to remain independent in the long term will be another critical indicator of China's commitment to the unique "One Country, Two Systems" model.

In addition, the legitimacy of Hong Kong's Chief Executive will be greatly enhanced if the promise of universal suffrage is fulfilled. By this I mean an election that provides the people of Hong Kong a meaningful choice of candidates representative of the voters' will. This means allowing for a competitive election in which a range of candidates with differing policy approaches are given an opportunity to seek the support of eligible Hong Kong voters.

That is why the administration has called on the PRC to uphold its commitments to Hong Kong under the Basic Law to preserve Hong Kong's freedoms and autonomy, including through universal suffrage. We encourage Beijing, the Hong Kong government and the people of Hong Kong to work together to advance Hong Kong's democratic development, establish universal suffrage by 2017, and preserve Hong Kong's autonomy and its free and open society.

Beijing's Decision and the Nominating Committee

Based on the Sino-British Joint Declaration and the Basic Law from 1997, in 2007 the Standing Committee of the National People's Congress (NPCSC) agreed that the election of Hong Kong's Chief Executive "may be implemented by the method of universal suffrage" in 2017. Over the last year, the people of Hong Kong, the Hong Kong government, and the authorities in Beijing have vigorously debated how that process should take place.

Early this year, the Hong Kong government held a first round of public consultations to discuss the implementation of universal suffrage for the 2017 election. Hong Kong residents submitted numerous suggestions for designing the electoral system and many Hong Kong residents voiced their desire for significant democratic reform. I visited Hong Kong in early May and met with a broad cross-section of the public, including representatives of civil society and various political parties, in addition to the head of the Legislative Council and senior officials in the Hong Kong government. I can attest to the vigorous and open debate in Hong Kong about how best to implement universal suffrage.

That debate intensified during the summer. Local NGOs conducted an online poll of public opinion in which almost 800,000 Hong Kong residents expressed pro-democracy views, and in early July, perhaps as many as 500,000 Hong Kong residents took part in the annual pro-democracy demonstration. The Hong Kong government in July submitted a report to Beijing based on its results of the public consultation and the NPCSC then issued its decision on August 31.

The NPCSC decision on August 31 set limits on the selection of the Chief Executive by universal suffrage. It limited the number of candidates to two or three, required the Chief Executive to be a person who "loves the country and loves Hong Kong," and mandated that any nominee must receive the endorsement of more than half of the 1,200 person nominating committee. While the NPCSC's decision conformed to requirements of the Basic Law in the literal sense, it was criticized by many Hong Kong groups and triggered the public protests that are still underway. The objection to the NPCSC decision of August 31 is that it would effectively block nonestablishment candidates from competing in the election for Chief Executive.

The Protests and the Hong Kong Government Response

On September 26, a week-long student strike and independently organized demonstrations against Beijing's decision escalated when a few dozen university students entered the grounds of Hong Kong government headquarters. When a crowd surged onto a major adjacent thoroughfare, Hong Kong police used tear gas to disperse the crowd. Rather than dispersing the protesters, however, the use of tear gas prompted more residents to take to the streets and protesters settled into three main protest locations.

On October 21, the Hong Kong government and leaders from the Hong Kong Federation of Students engaged in one round of televised talks, but there has been little dialogue reported between the two sides since. The Hong Kong government has complained that the protest movement lacks representative leadership it can negotiate with. Protesters have countered that the government is not taking their demands seriously.

Within the past 2 weeks, Hong Kong police have enforced civil court injunctions to clear certain protest sites. While there were some clashes between police and protesters in clearance operations in the Mongkok area, we assessed that both parties had for the most part acted with patience and restraint. The alarming flareup on November 30 near Hong Kong government offices demonstrates, however, that the potential for violence remains and that all sides need now more than ever to exercise restraint and to lower tensions.

Since these protests began in September, we have emphasized at all levels our support for freedom of peaceful assembly and freedom of expression without fear of retribution. We have encouraged the Hong Kong authorities and the protestors to address their differences through dialogue. We have urged the Hong Kong government to act with restraint and the protestors to express their views peacefully. We have also categorically denied allegations from China that the United States is in any way involved in the protests. It is disingenuous to suggest that this debate is driven by outsiders when it is so clearly about Hong Kongers' hopes for their future.

Next Steps

It is important to note that the electoral reform process in Hong Kong is still underway. Due to the protests, the Hong Kong government delayed a second round of public consultations, which are now expected to begin later this month. These consultations are meant to allow the public to provide input into how the nominating committee will be constituted and the mechanism by which candidates will be selected. It will be during this round of consultations that the government and the residents of Hong Kong explore options for devising a nominating system that can garner a sufficient number of votes to pass the legislature.

In order for electoral reforms to be implemented, a bill to amend the Basic Law must pass the Legislative Council with a two-thirds majority and be approved by Beijing. This legislative action is planned for the first half of 2015. If the Legislative Council does not amend the Basic Law by the summer of 2015, Beijing has said that the 2017 election for Chief Executive would again be carried out under the existing system under which the Chief Executive is selected by an Election Committee of 1,200 members rather than directly by Hong Kong's 5 million potentially eligible voters. This would be a significant setback to the democratization process, and it underscores the importance of the efforts by Hong Kong's authorities and its people to design an electoral process that maximizes progress toward universal suffrage under the Basic Law.

Conversely, if the Basic Law is amended to provide for a multicandidate selection process for the Chief Executive, 2017 will mark the first time in Hong Kong's history that its citizens will be given a voice in that choice. A multicandidate competitive election would be a major step in Hong Kong's, and indeed the People's Republic of China's, political development.

U.S. Interests and Actions

Mr. Chairman, allow me to describe the importance we place on our relationship with Hong Kong. This relationship rests on three pillars: shared values, economic and cultural relations, and people-to-people ties. Hong Kong has long reflected and protected fundamental freedoms: freedom of expression, freedom of peaceful assembly, a strong independent legal system, rule of law, a free media, and an active civil society—all values shared with the United States.

We are also linked by strong economic ties. Hong Kong is the ninth-largest market for U.S. exports and the sixth-largest market for U.S. agricultural products.

Despite Hong Kong's small population, our trade surplus with Hong Kong is our largest surplus with any single trading partner. More than 1,400 American companies have invested in and set up shop in Hong Kong. Hong Kong is a key source of foreign direct investment in the United States, as well. Hong Kong's world class financial markets, which include Asia's second-largest stock exchange and third-largest foreign exchange market, are supported by a transparent regulatory regime and strict oversight. Hong Kong is a strong voice in both APEC and the WTO in favor of free trade, often in alignment with our own goals.

This is possible because of Hong Kong's special status under the principle of "One Country, Two Systems" that allows Hong Kong to operate as a separate customs territory from China and exercise autonomy in areas other than foreign and defense affairs, including its judiciary system and its U.S. dollar-linked currency and financial system. This has allowed us to develop a robust relationship in law enforcement arenas—including export control, counterterrorism, counterproliferation, antimoney laundering, and anticorruption—in which Hong Kong's authorities work with the United States to protect our security interests. The United States has signed a wide range of agreements with Hong Kong since the handover, which provide for extensive technical cooperation in these and other areas. For example, Hong Kong counterparts respond positively to more than 95 percent of requests from U.S. Customs to search containers and the Hong Kong Customs and Excise Department has actively enforced the Convention on the International Trade in Endangered Species (CITES).

In addition, we have deep social, cultural, and people-to-people ties, boosted by the tens of thousands of U.S. citizens residing in Hong Kong, and the thousands more who visit Hong Kong, visa-free, every day for business or tourism. Hong Kong is one of the highest per capita sources in the world of foreign students in America's higher education system and hosts thousands of American students, academics, and journalists as well.

CONCLUSION

The United States and China each have a vested interest in Hong Kong's continued stability, autonomy, and prosperity. It is therefore important that China upholds its international obligations and commitments that Hong Kong's high degree of autonomy will be respected and nurtured. It is in all of our interests to see electoral reform in Hong Kong that provides the people of Hong Kong a meaningful choice of candidates, and that the 2017 elections in Hong Kong will be transparent, fair, and reflective of the opinions of the Hong Kong people.

We have also consistently counseled the Hong Kong government to exercise restraint and called on protesters to exercise their right to freedom of expression peacefully. We have consistently supported further dialogue between the government and protesters as the best way for Hong Kong to move this important debate forward. An open society that respects the rights of its citizens and universal freedoms, with the highest possible degree of autonomy and governed by the rule of law, is essential for Hong Kong's continued stability and prosperity.

We will continue to voice our support for universal suffrage in Hong Kong and to stand up for universal human rights and fundamental freedoms. We will stand up for Hong Kong's autonomy under "One Country, Two Systems" and the Basic Law. We will continue to encourage the government and people of Hong Kong to work together peacefully to advance Hong Kong's democratic development. We believe this engagement remains the most effective way to preserve Hong Kong's autonomy and free and open society.

Mr. Chairman, I thank you for the opportunity to appear before you today to discuss Hong Kong. I look forward to answering any questions you and others from the committee may have.

Senator CARDIN. Thank you, Secretary Russel, again, for all of your leadership on this issue.

As I pointed out, the 1992 United States-Hong Kong Policy Act, which acknowledged the separate identity of Hong Kong from mainland China and recognized the importance of Hong Kong as an economic partner of the United States and its global role in the economy, gave the President the ability to eliminate that status if it is not sufficiently autonomous to justify such treatment, and spelled out very clearly that human rights are of great importance to the United States and directly relevant to United States interests in Hong Kong. The 1984 Joint Declaration between Great Britain and China, "one country, two systems," contained in its index the International Covenant on Civil and Political Rights, which provides for universal suffrage. Then the 1990 China National People's Congress Declaration, the Basic Law for Hong Kong, spelled out the ultimate aim and selection of the Chief Executive by universal suffrage, upon the nomination by a broadly representative nominating committee in accordance with democratic procedures. They clearly are not following that with their most recent declaration on August 31.

The protests were peaceful. We had nothing to do with the protests, as you pointed out. The authorities exercised some restraint, but recently that changed.

My question to you is what action does the administration intend to take to communicate that their most recent action, on August 31, was unacceptable? And Congress is prepared to take action, which, among other things, reinstates our basic commitment to human rights, but also points out that the annual report on its progress will be reinstated, but also changing the burden from the administration having to certify that it is no longer in status to one where you have to certify that they are in status. Would that not be helpful in giving you additional leverage in being able to make it clear that their current policy is unacceptable?

Mr. RUSSEL. Thank you very much, Mr. Chairman, for those questions, and those very important questions.

We, too, were disappointed by the August 31 decision of the NPC. Now, our analysis suggests that this decision does not necessarily contravene the letter of the Basic Law, but the decision could and should have gone much, much further to allow for a nomination by a broadly representative nominating committee in accordance with democratic procedures.

Our logic is this. The legitimacy of the Chief Executive, which matters greatly, would be enhanced by a competitive electoral process that includes multiple candidates. Our objective is to encourage a process that culminates in universal suffrage, which allows the people of Hong Kong to have a meaningful say in the selection of the Chief Executive.

Now, the August 31 decision that you referenced circumscribes, to some extent, the nominating process. But, that process—how to define membership and the procedures of the nominating committee—is very much still underway, it is still a work in process. It is going to be the subject of a second round of public consultations that are expected to start later this month.

I would also add, Mr. Chairman, that, in our approach, which has been forceful and clear, we have taken care not to lose sight of the fact that this is an issue that will and should be decided by the people of Hong Kong. And they have demonstrated they are no pushovers. They have shown that they are willing to express their dissatisfaction and their aspirations directly to the authorities through responsible and peaceful dissent. I believe our role is to foster that and to shine a bright light on the situation and show that we support the rights of the people of Hong Kong.

So, you asked what we are doing about it. Well, first and foremost, we are speaking out very clearly and very forcefully. As I mentioned, I was in the room when President Obama stood next to Xi Jinping in Beijing and spoke forcefully about our support for the rights of the people of Hong Kong. I was in the room when Secretary Kerry stood next to the Chinese Foreign Minister in front of the cameras and said that we are concerned about the situation in Hong Kong because human rights are a centerpiece of American foreign policy. And I can attest, personally, to the fact that words matter, because I have been the target of considerable Chinese unhappiness about those words. We have their attention.

So, my points would be, one, Mr. Chairman, this situation is still playing out. It is far from over. And it would be a mistake to underestimate the resolve and the determination of the Hong Kong people. Two, the Chinese know that the world is watching. And this matters. It has a reputational cost to them.

With regard to the third part of your question concerning the prospect of legislation, I know that there is a discussion underway among our staffs about the specifics. In terms of the general principle, I would ask, Mr. Chairman, that nothing in the legislation should undermine the principle that Hong Kong is autonomous. We want to be careful not to lump Hong Kong and the mainland together in a way that undercuts inadvertently that autonomy, because Hong Kong's record in rule of law and economic freedoms is so important. I mentioned that Hong Kong scored number one on the Heritage Foundation's list of economic freedom. Well, what I did not mention is that the PRC ranks 137. These are different systems. And preserving the difference between these two systems should be an objective of any legislation.

Senator CARDIN. Thank you. I agree with you, words do matter. And I think the President's comments, the Secretary of State's comments, were strong and very appropriate. So, I agree with you. But, I think actions are also important. And we are concerned about how the protesters are going to be treated, because we know there are some legal issues that are now pending, some orders that are currently pending, and I would hope that we will watch very carefully how the legal system of Hong Kong deals with the individuals that were peacefully demonstrating. And I can tell you that this Senator is going to be watching that very closely as it could have major impact on action that I propose to take in the next Congress.

And then, just the last point I would make, I think it is very clear the commitment that China made for Hong Kong to be able to implement universal suffrage. And we acknowledge the autonomy of Hong Kong, but it appears very clear to us that China is influencing the implementation of universal suffrage in a way that is inconsistent with the commitment they gave to respect the International Covenant on Civil and Political Rights. And it has been, now, 30 years since the Joint Declaration. We have passed enough time that this is a critical milestone as to whether Hong Kong indeed will embrace democratic principles.

With that, I turn to Senator Rubio.

Senator RUBIO. Thank you. Thank you, Mr. Chairman, for holding this hearing.

And thank you for being here today.

I wanted to ask you, right off the bat, on September 29, the U.S. consulate general in Hong Kong issued a statement. Here is what it said, in part, ''We do not take sides in the discussions of Hong Kong's political development, nor do we support any particular individuals or groups involved in it.'' Does that reflect the official position of this administration? That we do not take sides?

Mr. RUSSEL. Well, thank you, Mr. Ranking Member, Senator Rubio. I did not get a chance to express my appreciation for your work, your leadership, and your support on this subcommittee.

The statement issued by the consulate in September, which is one of a long series of public statements by U.S. officials, was aimed at eradicating a story that was topping the news in Hong Kong, suggesting that the United States was the hidden hand behind a particular group or a particular individual involved in the demonstrations. The fact of the matter is, Senator, we do take sides. We take the side of justice. We take the side of freedom. We take the side of dialogue. We take the side of freedom of speech and freedom of assembly. We take the side of peaceful protest. We do not take sides with an individual or a particular group.

But, if you look at our statements, the statements of the U.S. Government, the President, the Secretary of State, and the consulate, you will see a consistent and clear message of support for the principle of universal suffrage in line with the Basic Law, support for the democratic aspirations of the people of Hong Kong, and, importantly, support for "one country, two systems." We believe that the United States has a stake in preserving the unique character and system of Hong Kong. That is a system that has, as I mentioned before you came in, the number one spot in the Heritage Foundation's Index of Economic Freedom. That counts for a lot.

Similarly, we strongly support the process to apply universal suffrage to the selection of the Chief Executive in 2017. And by "universal suffrage," we do not mean a very narrowly constructed arrangement, we mean giving voice to the citizens of Hong Kong, giving them a say in the selection of their leader.

Senator RUBIO. Yes. Well, thank you for that explanation. That clarifies most of that. But, I did want to ask you this, then. On the 31st of August, China's National People's Conference—and I am going to read from it just to make sure that I get it right—it placed strict conditions, as has been talked about here. And here is one of the things that they said about the—that the Deputy Secretary General said, the candidates would need to, "love the country"— I imagine meaning China—"and also love Hong Kong."

So, I wonder if that—by that term, of "loving the country," is basically code for loving the—having loyalty to the Chinese Communist Party. And so, my question is, Is it the position of this administration that the August decision, with regard to the nature of this election, is in keeping with the aims and the requirements of article 45 of the Basic Law? Are the Chinese compliant with that in their position that they have taken?

Mr. RUSSEL. Well, thank you for that question, Senator.

We were disappointed by the August 31 decision. We think that that formula excessively circumscribes the selection process that will be an essential element of the application of universal suffrage. Our analysis suggests that, while that decision of the National People's Congress may not literally contravene the letter of the basic agreement, it falls very far short of the aspirations of the people of Hong Kong, and it falls short of what we would hope for, in terms of a nomination process that would result in a broadly representative nominating committee, in accordance with democratic procedures.

The key point, Senator, is, we believe that, for the purposes of Hong Kong's long-term stability and prosperity, the legitimacy of the Chief Executive will be greatly enhanced by a credible application of universal suffrage that allows a free expression of choice by the voters to select from among competing points of view, not simply a choice between three identical handpicked candidates. And this is what is under discussion now among the stakeholders in Hong Kong.

I visited Hong Kong in May and found a very vibrant debate between nongovernmental groups, between political parties, between the Hong Kong authorities, and, obviously, representatives of Beijing. That debate has intensified. It has spilled out onto the streets. It has taken the form of major referenda and questionnaires. And, later this month, we expect and hope that it will again take the form of a second round of public consultations.

So, we consider this still a work in progress, and it is our determination, as an administration, to speak out and have America's voice——

Senator RUBIO. But, to summarize your——

Mr. RUSSEL [continuing]. Very clearly——

Senator RUBIO [continuing]. Summarize your statement—and I appreciate your answer—but, to summarize it is that perhaps they have found a technical way to, at a minimum, be semicompliant with the letter of law, but certainly fall well short of the spirit of the law, in——

Mr. RUSSEL. That is our view.

Senator RUBIO [continuing]. Regards to how it is been written.

Well, in that sense, then, is there not a couple of lessons to be taken from this? The first is that the Chinese Government has proven to be an untrustworthy ally—or an untrustworthy partner, in any sort of future—or international agreements. I mean, they basically signed this agreement, and now have found interesting ways to circumvent it, certainly in its application or how it is working, as you said, in the spirit of it. What does that say about their future reliability in any other agreement they enter into with us, with the international community, with anyone?

Mr. RUSSEL. Senator——

Senator RUBIO [continuing]. At a minimum, it calls into question their reliability.

Mr. RUSSEL. Senator, there is no question but that the United States, the region, and the world is watching how China deals with Hong Kong and how it implements its commitments under the Basic Law and other agreements. That is why we have been urging and counseling the Chinese, both privately and publicly, to exercise restraint, to be flexible, and to allow the voices of the people of Hong Kong to be heard.

Their neighbors are drawing conclusions also about China and about the reliability of China's pledges and commitments. I do not think that there is a case that can fairly be made to describe this August 31 decision by the NPC as in direct contravention of the Basic Law, but I equally believe there is not a credible case that would allow us to argue that the August 31 decision furthered the cause of universal suffrage.

Senator CARDIN. Senator Rubio has one additional question, but I just really want to underscore one point of urgency here.

You point out that the region is watching, the world is watching. And you are absolutely correct. Hong Kong is very important economically, not just to the United States bilaterally, but it is a part of the economic fiber of global commerce. So, there is a great deal of interest in what is happening. But, when you see what happened in the Taiwan elections, you know that it has political consequences, at least the analysis is that it had an impact on the results in Taiwan's elections. When you look at British parliamentarians being denied visas to look at the country to see if they are in compliance with agreements, that raises questions as to whether China's taken taken this to a different level.

So, I would just underscore the urgency of a strategy that includes more than just words as it relates to the autonomy and our relationship with Hong Kong.

And Senator Rubio has one additional question.

Senator RUBIO. I just would make the comment, I think you can make the argument that how you apply a law directly contradicts its meaning, even if—maybe what they are saying and what they are doing, here, are two separate things. They clearly want to influence the outcome of this election toward—they clearly want to set up a process that would elect someone that will do their bidding and will be compliant to the wishes of the Central Government in China. And that is in direct contradiction to an agreement that was based upon true autonomy.

And so, I do believe it is in direct contravention of the agreement. I, furthermore, would say that, you know, there have been statements—I am sorry—there have—there has been evidence that these groups of armed thugs who miraculously showed up out of nowhere to beat up these protesters—I think the evidence is pretty clear that they were sent there by the Central Government, at least in my opinion. And I would love to see someone disprove that. So, I think that you have to look at that, as well, as a factor in all of this.

But, here is my final point. I think that the learning—the lesson to be learned by all of this is that all this talk out there, that the hopes that—you know, these economic interchanges and dialogue with China was going to change the nature of the Central Government, is a fairytale. It is wishful thinking. This government, as it is currently structured in China, is—this is their nature, is to control, to be authoritarian. And every instance in which they have been challenged in that, or have been challenged toward more of a democratic or a societal opening, they have pushed back against. And Hong Kong is the latest example of it. And I think there is a lesson to be learned there, that if we are hanging our hopes that more economic interchange with them is going to somehow transform them into a more open, more liberalized, and more inclusive government, it does not seem that way at this point, certainly from their reaction with what has happened in Hong Kong. And I think that that is a factor that we need to accept today as a reality, and base our policy based on that reality, because this does not leave me hopeful that this is a government that, at any point in the near future, is going to be more open and more accommodating. In fact, it is the tactics of a government that is becoming increasingly more centralized, more authoritarian, and more willing to take strong actions against those who challenge the authority of the Communist Party and the Central Government. And I think that bodes ill for the future of the region, and, quite frankly, of the world, as China takes on a greater economic and military importance.

Senator CARDIN. Thank you, Senator Rubio.

Secretary Russel, once again, I personally thank you for the courtesy, respect, and expertise that you shared with this subcommittee during the past 2 years. It has been a very open relationship, with very frank discussions. As a result, I think the United States spoke with greater strength in our messages to East Asia and the Pacific. So, thank you very much. And with that, you are excused.

Mr. RUSSEL. Thank you very much, Chairman.

Senator CARDIN. Our second panel is Dr. Richard Bush, director, Center for Northeast Asian Policy Studies, Chen-Fu and Cecilia Yen Koo Chair of Taiwan Studies, senior fellow in foreign policy, the Brookings Institute; and Dr. Sophie Richardson, the China director, Human Rights Watch, Washington, DC.

Our witnesses have agreed that their written statements will be incorporated in our record, and they are open to us proceeding directly with questioning. And I appreciate that very much. And, as I said earlier, we may have some additional written questions for the record.

[The prepared statements of Dr. Bush and Dr. Richardson follow:]

PREPARED STATEMENT OF RICHARD C. BUSH

There has been a wide range of views in Hong Kong about the value of democratic elections.

So far, the Chinese Government has consistently chosen to engineer the Hong Kong electoral system so that no individual it mistrusts could be elected Chief Executive (CE) and no political coalition that it fears could win control of the Legislative Council (or LegCo). To elect the Chief Executive, it created an election committee composed mainly of people it trusts. For LegCo, it established functional constituencies that give special representation to establishment economic and social groups. These functional constituencies together pick half the members of LegCo. As a result, Hong Kong's economic elite has dominated those institutions.

Major economic interests in Hong Kong have been happy with the current setup because it provides them with privileged access to decisionmaking and the ability to block initiatives proposed by the democratic camp. Within this establishment, there is long-standing belief that majority rule would create irresistible demands for a welfare state, which would raise taxes on corporations and wealthy individuals and so sap Hong Kong's competitiveness.

The public, on the other hand, supports democratization. In the most representative election races (for some LegCo seats), candidates of the pro-democracy parties together get 55 to 60 percent of the vote. Those parties have tried for over 20 years to make the electoral system more representative and to eliminate the ability of Beijing and the establishment to control political outcomes. But there are divisions within the pan-democratic camp between moderate and radical factions, based on the degree of mistrust of Beijing's intentions.

There is a working class party and a labor confederation that supports Beijing and is supported by it. On electoral reform, it has followed China's lead.

Of course, any electoral system requires the protection of political rights. The Joint Declaration and the Hong Kong Basic Law protected those rights on paper, and the judiciary generally has upheld them. But there are serious concerns in Hong Kong that political rights are now being whittled away.

The August 31 decision of the PRC National People's Congress-Standing Committee on the 2017 Chief Executive election confirmed the fears of Hong Kong's pan-democratic camp that Beijing does not intend to create a genuinely democratic electoral system. That decision almost guaranteed there would be with some kind of public protest.

Before August 31, there had been some hope in Hong Kong that China's leaders would set flexible parameters for the 2017 election of the Chief Executive, flexible enough to allow an election in which candidates that represented the range of local opinions could compete on a level playing field. Instead, the rules the Standing Committee of the National People's Congress laid down were interpreted as ensuring that Beijing and the local Hong Kong establishment, by controlling the nominating committee, could screen out candidates that they saw as a threat to their interests.

I happen to believe that before August 31 there was available a compromise on the nomination process. The approach I have in mind would have liberalized the composition of the nominating committee so that it was more representative of Hong Kong society and set a reasonable threshold for placing someone in nomination. This would have been consistent with the Basic Law (a Chinese requirement) and likely ensured that a pan-Democratic politician could have been nominated (the democrats' minimum hope). Hong Kong voters would have had a genuine choice. There were Hong Kong proposals along these lines. Such an approach would have had a chance of gaining the support of moderate Democrats in Legislative Council, enough for reaching the two-thirds majority required for passage of the election plan.

Reaching such a compromise was difficult because of the deep-seated mistrust between the Hong Kong democratic camp and Beijing, and within the democratic camp. If there was to be movement toward a deal Beijing would have had to signal that it was serious about such a compromise, in order to engage moderate democrats. It chose not to, and an opportunity was lost.

Why Beijing spurned a compromise is unclear.

Perhaps it interpreted its "universal suffrage" pledge narrowly, to mean one-person-one-vote, and not a competitive election. Perhaps it wished to defer a truly competitive contest until it was sure that one-person-one-vote elections would not hurt its interests. Perhaps Beijing was overly frightened about the proposed civil disobedience campaign called "Occupy Central." Perhaps it judged that radical democrats would block their moderate comrades from agreeing to a compromise. Perhaps China actually believed its own propaganda that "foreign forces" were behind the protests. Perhaps it never had any intention of allowing truly representative government and majority rule. But if Beijing believed that taking a hard line would ensure stability, it was badly mistaken.

Whatever the case, the majority in Hong Kong saw the August 31 decision as a bait-and-switch way for Beijing to continue to control the outcome of the CE election and as a denial of the long-standing desire for genuine democracy. A coalition of student leaders, Occupy Central supporters, democratic politicians, radical activists, and middle-class people resorted to the only political outlet they had: public protest. If the Chinese Government had wished to empower Hong Kong radicals, it couldn't have hit upon a better way.

Although Beijing's August 31 decision guaranteed a public response in Hong Kong, the form it took was unexpected. Student groups preempted the original Occupy Central plan, and the takeover of three separate downtown areas resulted, not from a plan but from the flow of events. The Hong Kong Police did overreact in some instances, but each time it sought to reestablish control, there was a surge of public support for the core protester groups, mobilized by social and other media.

The protests were fueled by more than a desire for democracy.

Also at work were factors common in other advanced societies. Hong Kong's level of income and wealth inequality is one of the highest in the world. Young people tend to believe that they will not be able to achieve a standard of living similar to that of their parents. Real wages have been flat for more than a decade. Buying a home is out of reach for young people, in part because a small group of real estate companies control the housing supply. Smart and ambitious individuals from China compete for good jobs.

Hong Kong students have gotten the most attention in the current protests. Just as important however, are older cohorts who are pessimistic about their life chances. They believe that the Hong Kong elite, which controls both economic and political power, is to blame for these problems. They regard genuine democracy as the only remedy.

The Hong Kong government's response has been mixed but restrained on the whole.

The Hong Kong police did commit excesses in their attempt to control the crowds. Teargas was used once early on, and pepper spray on a number of occasions since then. There was one particular incident where police officers beat a protester excessively (for which seven of the officers involved were arrested last week).

It is worth noting that the scenario for which the police prepared was not the one that occurred. What was expected was a civil disobedience action in a relatively restricted area with a moderate number of protesters who, following their leaders' plan, would allow themselves to be arrested. What happened in late September was very different. There were three venues instead of one. Many more protesters took part, and they had no interest in quickly offering themselves for arrest. Instead, they sought to maintain control of public thoroughfares, a violation of law, until Beijing and the Hong Kong government made major concessions. Even when courts have ordered some streets cleared, those occupying have not always complied.

After the initial clashes, the Hong Kong government chose not to mount a major crackdown but instead to wait out the protesters. It accepted the occupation for a number of weeks, and now seeks to clear some streets pursuant to court order. Moreover, the government undertook to engage at least one of the students in a dialogue over how to end the crisis. In the only session of the dialogue to occur, on October 21, senior officials floated ideas to assuage some of the protesters' concerns and to improve upon the electoral parameters laid down by Beijing.

The dialogue has not progressed for two reasons. First of all, the Hong Kong government is not a free agent in resolving the crisis. Beijing is the ultimate decider here, and the Hong Kong government must stay within the guidelines it sets. Second, the student federation leaders who took part in the dialogue are not free agents either. They represent only one of the student groups, and other actors are involved. With its leadership fragmented, the movement has never figured out its minimum goals and therefore what it would accept in return for ending the protest. It underestimated Beijing's resolve and instead has insisted on the impossible, that Beijing withdraw the August 31 decision. Now, even though the Hong Kong public and the leaders of the original Occupy Central effort believe that the protesters should retire to contend another day, the occupation continues.

For those who believe that the rule of law is a fundamental pillar of Hong Kong's autonomy, the last 2 months have been worrisome. Once some members of a community decide for themselves which laws they will obey and which they won't; once the authorities pick and choose which laws they will enforce and abide by, the rule of law begins to atrophy. The protesters' commitment to democracy is commendable. The generally restrained and peaceable character of their protest has been widely praised. But something is lost when both the community and its government begins to abandon the idea that no one is above the law.

Regional views implications: Observers have believed that the implications of the Umbrella Movement are greatest for Taiwan, because Beijing has said that Taiwan will be reunified under the same formula that it used for Hong Kong (one-country, two systems). And there was momentary media attention in Taiwan when the Hong Kong protests began, but it quickly dissipated. The vast majority of Taiwan citizens have long since rejected one-country, two systems. China's Hong Kong policies only reconfirm what Taiwan people already knew.

Hong Kong events also send a signal to all of East Asia's democracies, not just Taiwan. Anyone who studies Hong Kong's politics and society comes to the conclusion that it has been as ready for democracy as any place in East Asia, and that its instability in recent years is due more to the absence of democracy than because it is unready.

The long-standing premise of U.S. policy is that Hong Kong people are ready for democracy. Since the protest movement began, the U.S. Government has reiterated its support for the rule of law, Hong Kong's autonomy, respect for the political freedoms of Hong Kong people, and a universal-suffrage election that would provide the people of Hong Kong "a genuine choice of candidates that are representative of the peoples and the voters' will." Washington has also called for restraint on all sides.

Finally, the strategic question for East Asia is what the rise of China means for its neighbors. That question will be answered in part by China's power relative to the United States and others. But it will also be answered by what happens between China and its neighbors in a series of specific encounters. Through those interactions, China will define what kind of great power it will become. North Korea, the East and South China Seas, and Taiwan are the most obvious of these specific encounters. But Hong Kong is as well. If the struggle there for a more democratic system ends well, it will tell us something positive about China's future trajectory. If it ends badly, it will say something very different.

Looking forward, several options exist for resolving the crisis and only one of them is good.

One option is a harsh crackdown by China. Article 18 of the Basic Law gives Beijing the authority to declare a state of emergency in Hong Kong if "turmoil" there "endangers national unity or security and is beyond the control" of the Hong Kong government. In that case, Chinese national laws would be applied to Hong Kong and could be enforced in the same way they are in China. We would then see crowd control, Chinese style. I believe this scenario is unlikely as long as Beijing has some confidence that the protest movement will become increasingly isolated and ultimately collapse.

A second option is that the occupation ends but the unrepresentative electoral system that has been used up until now continues. That would happen because two-thirds of the Legislative Council is required to enact the one-person-one-vote proposal of the Chinese and Hong Kong governments for electing the Chief Executive. Getting two-thirds requires the votes of a few democratic members. If all moderate democrats oppose the package for whatever reason, then the next CE will be elected by the 1,200-person election committee, not by Hong Kong voters. Protests are liable to resume. There is a danger that in response, Beijing will move quietly to restrict press freedom, the rule of law, and the scope for civil society beyond what it has already done.

The third scenario is for a late compromise within the parameters of Beijing's August 31 decision. The goal here would be to create a process within the nominating committee that would make it possible for a leader of the democratic camp to be nominated for the Chief Executive election, creating a truly competitive election. That requires two things. First, the nominating committee must be more representative of Hong Kong society. Second, the nominating committee, before it picks the two or three election nominees, should be able to review a greater number of potential nominees. Done properly, that could yield the nomination of a democratic politician whom Beijing does not mistrust but whose platform would reflect the aspirations of democratic voters. Prominent individuals in Hong Kong have discussed this approach in print, and Hong Kong senior officials have hinted a willingness to consider it. For such a scenario to occur, Beijing would have to be willing to show more flexibility than demonstrated so far; the Hong Kong government should be forthcoming about what it has in mind; and some leaders of the democratic camp must be willing to engage both Beijing and the Hong Kong government. In the climate of mutual mistrust that has deepened since August 31, that is a tall order. But at this point it appears to be the best way out of a bad situation.

PREPARED STATEMENT OF DR. SOPHIE RICHARDSON

Mr. Chairman, Ranking Member Rubio, and distinguished members of the subcommittee, thank you for inviting me to testify today. As protestors remain on the streets of Hong Kong, this discussion is timely, and we hope to clarify the critical human rights issues at stake.

It is appropriate to recall that in 1997 the hope was that not only would Hong Kong's autonomy be respected, and the rights to the freedom of assembly, expression, and political participation there would remain intact, but also that these realities might have a positive effect on the mainland. People in Hong Kong have continued to make clear how much they value an independent judiciary, a free press, a meritocratic civil service, and a professional police force. Yet developments of the past year have shown that in fact, the mainland's politics and disdain for rights are having alarming consequences for those realities, a territory of critical importance to the United States and within the region.

Since 1997, Human Rights Watch has expressed concern over erosions of Hong Kong's autonomy, particularly with respect to the independence of the press, increased interference into Hong Kong politics, and a growing role for Beijing's Central Liaison Office in Hong Kong. Consistent with its attitude toward other regions on its periphery from Tibet to Taiwan, President Xi Jinping's government appears to perceive Hong Kong people's greater demands for a fully elected government— one that responds to their concerns and one in which they are entitled to according to law—as an existential threat. Beijing has insisted that the Chief Executive must be someone who passes a political litmus test set by the Chinese Communist Party, has made clear that efforts by people in Hong Kong to press their demands through every possible peaceful avenue will be rejected, and has moved swiftly to crush any expressions of sympathy in the mainland for pro-democracy efforts in Hong Kong.

The extraordinary demonstrations by a cross-section of people in Hong Kong are in turn not simply about the composition of Hong Kong's nomination committee. After waiting patiently for years for China to fulfill its promise to give democracy, many are angry at the central government's overreach, particularly with respect to its decision to retain control over the selection of Hong Kong's leader. Many expressed growing frustration and a sense of marginalization by the Hong Kong government, arguing that it increasingly failed to respond to the interests of the majority on issues ranging from education policy to urban planning. They are also a reaction to threats to key independent institutions in the territory that have helped protect human rights, and to growing unease over whether the Hong Kong government is serving the interests of the Hong Kong people or the central government when it comes to key decisions. In the broadest sense, the current tensions are local and logical reactions of people who have enjoyed civil liberties, an independent judiciary, a free press, and a reasonably responsive government, but who see these freedoms increasingly threatened, and who have some sense of how these rights are denied just across the border.

BEIJING'S LEGAL OBLIGATIONS WITH RESPECT TO HONG KONG

The 1984 Sino-British Joint Declaration spells out the terms for transfer of Hong Kong from British to Chinese control. That document stipulates that Hong Kong shall have "a high degree of autonomy" in matters other than national defense and foreign policy, while the Basic Law, Hong Kong's functional constitution, states that universal suffrage is the "ultimate aim" for the selection of the Chief Executive, the top leader, as well as members of the Legislative Council. The Basic Law also provides that the International Covenant on Civil and Political Rights (ICCPR) applies to Hong Kong, and the Covenant's guarantee of universal and equal suffrage means that people not only have the right to vote in elections, but also that they should have the right to stand for elections regardless of their political views. The committee responsible for monitoring the implementation of the ICCPR has also stated that when the law requires a certain threshold of supporters for nomination, "this requirement should be reasonable and not act as a barrier to candidacy."

Hong Kong's Basic Law states that Hong Kong can move toward the goal of universal suffrage by amending the electoral methods in three steps. First, two-thirds of all Legislative Council members have to endorse the amendments. Second, the current Chief Executive has to agree to it. Lastly, the amendments have to be reported to China's Standing Committee for the National Peoples' Congress (NPCSC) for approval.

The central government, in a series of decisions made since 1997, has backtracked on this obligation to institute universal and equal suffrage. The commitment to allowing electoral reform to be decided by Hong Kong people was first broken on April 6, 2004, when the NPCSC made an "interpretation" of the Basic Law adding a requirement that the Chief Executive submit a report to Beijing justifying the need for any further democratization. The decision shifted the initiative in proposing electoral reforms to Beijing's hand-picked Chief Executive, and away from the Legislative Council. In April 2004, directly after this NPCSC decision, the Chief Executive submitted a report that downplayed the need for substantial reform, and the NPCSC quickly followed this with a decision that ruled out universal suffrage for the 2007 selection of the Chief Executive and the selection of the 2008 Legislative Council.

In 2007, it ruled again that there would not be universal suffrage for the next elections of the Chief Executive and the Legislative Council in 2012. However, the 2007 decision also said that universal suffrage was "maybe" in store for the next Chief Executive election and Legislative Council elections in 2017 and 2020, respectively.

RECENT DEVELOPMENTS

As Hong Kong authorities began in late 2013 to prepare for a public consultation on how the 2017 elections should be carried out, Li Fei, a top mainland official and chairman of Beijing's Basic Law Committee, gave a speech stating that Hong Kong's Chief Executive must be an individual who "loves the country and loves Hong Kong," and that people who "confront the central government" do not meet this criterion. This followed similar pronouncements by Li's predecessor, Qiao Xiaoyang, as well as the director of the Liaison Office of the Chinese Government in Hong Kong, Zhang Xiaoming. Li added that the nomination committee for the Chief Executive would be restricted to a small selected group of Hong Kong people who will make a "collective" decision on candidates allowed to run in the election. The position countered earlier proposals by pro-democracy groups advocating a process in which all Hong Kong voters would be considered "members" of the nominating committee and candidates securing a specified number of public nominations would get on the ballot.

Over the subsequent months, the Hong Kong government and large parts of the public made their views clear about democracy and about Hong Kong's future. In early June 2014—shortly after the 25th anniversary of the Tiananmen Massacre— the Chinese Government issued a "white paper" asserting "overall jurisdiction" over Hong Kong, and that Hong Kong "is limited to the level of autonomy granted by the central leadership." This was widely seen as a violation of the commitment to "one country, two systems" in which Hong Kong would be granted "a high degree of autonomy," except in foreign affairs and defense. While the substance of the "white paper" was not new, and carries no legal weight, its timing and language were seen as abrasive and unnecessary by many in Hong Kong.

In late June 2014, more than 700,000 Hong Kong people—one in five registered voters—participated in an unofficial, nonbinding referendum to choose among three proposals for political reform that ensure universal suffrage via the pro-democracy "Occupy Central with Love and Peace" movement. The central government dismissed this effort as illegal and the product of "anti-China forces." In mid-July, Hong Kong Chief Executive (CE) Leung Chun-ying submitted the results of the government's public consultation to the central government, claiming it was "mainstream opinion" that a subsequent CE "love China and love Hong Kong," that the power to nominate CE candidates should remain vested in a committee controlled by Beijing, and that the legislature should not be democratized before the 2017 elections. The results of the public consultation as presented to the central Chinese Government were clearly manipulated, and failed to reflect different views articulated by large segments of the population.

Following the report's submission, on August 31, 2014, the NPCSC handed down its decision, which catalyzed the Occupy demonstrations: while it would allow all eligible voters in Hong Kong to cast ballots for the territory's Chief Executive, it would impose a stringent screening mechanism that effectively bars candidates the central government in Beijing dislikes from nomination for Chief Executive.

In reaction to the Chinese Government's August 31 rejection of open nominations for Hong Kong's Chief Executive, Occupy Central protest leaders, pan-democrats, and student protest leaders vowed to launch an "era of civil disobedience." Students boycotted classes between September 22 and 26; as that boycott came to a close, a group of students entered Civic Square, in front of the government headquarters in Admiralty, without permission. Police surrounded the students, and arrested and pepper sprayed some of them. The police treatment of the students provoked a large number of people—about 50,000—to congregate around Civic Square on September 27. "Occupy Central" organizers then announced that they were officially launching their planned demonstrations.

On September 28, Hong Kong police declared the protest illegal, and cordoned off the government headquarters grounds. The announcement drew even more protesters, who demanded access to the government headquarters. After an hours long standoff with police, protesters walked out onto a major thoroughfare that separated them from government headquarters. Police responded with pepper spray, batons, and 87 cans of tear gas. Protesters refused to disperse, and by the next morning they had occupied three sites in Hong Kong. For weeks, two of these sites remained occupied by hundreds of protesters, despite repeated police clearances, and assaults by persons opposing the Occupy movement. After police cleared one site in Mongkok on November 26, protesters responded with "fluid occupation" which involves repeatedly "crossing roads" slowly along the stretch of the former occupy sites to temporarily block traffic, as well as a failed escalation on November 30 to block all access to government headquarters in Admiralty.

HUMAN RIGHTS CONCERNS

Human Rights Watch has a host of concerns about human rights violations in Hong Kong, both specific to the protests and to larger issues.

On the core issue of electoral arrangements, the Basic Law guarantees the continued application of the International Covenant on Civil and Political Rights to Hong Kong, which in turn guarantees that people shall not only have the right to vote in elections, but also that they should have the right to stand for elections regardless of their political views. While the August 31 NPCSC decision will expand the vote to choose the Chief Executive to all eligible voters, it retains central government control over the nominating committee that will determine who may run as a candidate for Chief Executive. As recently as October 23, 2014, the U.N.'s Human Rights Committee expressed concern that the proposed nomination process poses "unreasonable restrictions" on the right to run.

The protests themselves have involved a number of human rights violations.

- Mainland and Hong Kong authorities deemed the protests illegal because organizers had not obtained permission under the Public Order Ordinance. Yet this Ordinance is in tension with international law because it imposes significant restrictions on the freedom of assembly without considering the importance of the right to gather to express grievances, and is susceptible to political abuse.

- The Hong Kong police's use of force, including tear gas and pepper spray, against unarmed protestors is of deep concern. While we note as positive Chief Executive Leung's condemnation of violence against protestors on October 4, and the arrest of seven police in late November for their brutal beating on October 16 of a peaceful demonstrator, the October 6 statement by the Chief Executive that authorities would use "all actions necessary" and evidence of further incidents involving excessive use of force by the police have undermined public confidence in the strict adherence of the police to the U.N. Basic Principles on the Use of Force and Firearms. Human Rights Watch calls on the Hong Kong government to conduct an independent investigation into police conduct during the protests.
- We are similarly deeply concerned about arrests of peaceful protestors at the beginning of the demonstrations in late September, but also during the late November efforts to clear protestors from particular locations, including the arrests of student demonstration leaders Joshua Wong and Lester Shum.
- We are also concerned that protesters appear to be subject to various types of intrusive surveillance by both the Hong Kong and Chinese governments, which apparently have based decisions to arrest protest leaders and bar others from entering China on their online postings and participation in the protests. The sense of pervasive collection and monitoring of participation in public debates and protests have thrown a pall over Hong Kong's robust civil liberties.

LARGER IMPLICATIONS

The central and Hong Kong government's failures to engage meaningfully with popular demands for greater democracy in the territory—through a formal consultation process, through a civic referendum, through months of peaceful demonstrations—leaves a longtime bastion of respect for rule of law on edge.

Beijing has made its disdain for the views of people in Hong Kong clear through its extraordinary overreach regarding autonomy, electoral arrangements, and a host of other policy issues. And because the Chinese Communist Party cannot countenance the idea that people in China might actually want participatory governance, it has repeatedly dismissed the demonstrations as a product of external, "anti-China forces."

It has also made clear that it will not tolerate any expressions of support in the mainland for the demonstrators in Hong Kong. More than 100 individuals have been detained in the mainland in recent months for doing as little as posting pictures of themselves holding a sign expressing support for Hong Kong people's demand for genuine universal suffrage. Beijing's unwillingness to allow student leaders or those sympathetic to the demonstrations from Hong Kong into the mainland is an utterly anachronistic and counterproductive strategy for dealing with the concerns there.

None of this bodes well for expectations that China will comply with key international legal obligations, come to grips with peaceful dissent, or accept—for Hong Kong, for Tibet, or for Xinjiang—the idea that many successful governments around the world have officials and administrations from regions benefiting from autonomy arrangements with views divergent from those at the national level. It is also an ominous sign for Hong Kong as a critical space for activists and organizations that work on or monitor developments in China. The efforts of nonviolent protestors in Hong Kong has also triggered expressions of concern across the region, prompting reactions from Tokyo, which rarely speaks publicly about human rights concerns in China, and from Taiwan, where voters appear to have been particularly motivated to reject a government arguing for closer ties to Beijing.

U.S. RESPONSE

The United States has expressed concern about violence against and by demonstrators, about the right to peaceful assembly, and the rights to vote and to run, and officials have said they have expressed these concerns directly to the highest levels of the Chinese Government. Some U.S. commentary, such as the initial statement regarding the August 31 NPCSC interpretation, did not accurately characterize the problem, while other remarks are superficially sensible—calling, for example, that differences be addressed through peaceful dialogue—but seem to deny the reality that Hong Kong peoples' efforts to do just that have been ignored. President Obama's comments on Hong Kong while in Beijing were so calibrated as to be convoluted, and he and other U.S. officials have repeated so frequently that the United States has had no role in fomenting or sustaining the demonstrations that it seems more concerned in assuaging Beijing's irrational fears than in standing up robustly for democratic rights.

We believe the U.S.' response to be factually accurate but functionally and diplomatically ineffective. It makes the mistake of focusing disproportionately on the reactions of the Chinese Government while forgetting to demonstrate solidarity with those on the front lines of a struggle for democracy. It is appropriate to ask why President Obama could be so publicly restrained on the topics of elections and democracy in Beijing yet a few days later offer up extensive commentary and support on the same subject in Burma, and shortly after in Australia. One thinks about visible gestures of solidarity for democracy elsewhere—for example, U.S. Assistant Secretary of State Victoria Nuland handing out bread to demonstrators in Maidan Square, American ambassadors observing elections (or expressing concerns about those elections' shortcomings) in other parts of Asia, or the U.S. vociferously decrying the rollbacks of democratic rights in other parts of the world. Why not Hong Kong?

To be so reticent has three problematic consequences. It undermines the very purpose of the U.S.-Hong Kong Policy Act, and it enables other governments, which for better or for worse take their cues on these issues from the U.S., to remain virtually silent. Arguably most problematic, it telegraphs to pro-democracy activists in Hong Kong and the mainland that they can likely only count on perfunctory support or recognition from the United States.

RECOMMENDATIONS

Physically removing demonstrators from the streets of Hong Kong will do little to answer their underlying grievances, and arguably will serve to exacerbate them. Already tensions between protesters and police have risen to a breaking point. The most critical and urgent step the central and Hong Kong governments can take is to revisit the territory's undemocratic electoral arrangements and ensure that appropriate ones are fashioned—as required by article 45 of the Basic Law—"in light of the actual situation," where the majority favors genuine democracy. We urge that both take immediate action, including by developing a time-bound and detailed plan, to put into practice universal and equal suffrage. Both should ensure that any proposals for nominations for the 2017 chief executive elections conform to international human rights standards, including those set out in the ICCPR. Any committee established for nominating candidates for the elections should conform to such requirements.

While it is reassuring to a point to see Hong Kong authorities investigate several police officers who were caught on camera viciously beating a protestor, that confidence is undermined by repeated incidents of excessive use of force. In just the past few days police have appeared to use excessive force in arresting student protest leaders Joshua Wong and Lester Shum on November 26 in Mong Kok as they stood by observing police; no warning or peaceful request to surrender to authorities were issued before police tackled them to the ground. In Admiralty and Mong Kok in the past 48 hours police have used pepper spray at close range after tearing off demonstrators' protective goggles, and used batons to hit people who were clearly trying to leave these areas. The authorities should meet with protest leaders, given that the single discussion held in October yielded no results. Hong Kong authorities should submit a new report to the central government acknowledging broad support for genuine democracy and ask the NPCSC to clarify or retract its August 31 decision to make the nomination committee for the Chief Executive genuinely "broadly representative," as articulated in the Basic Law. The Hong Kong authorities should also take steps to further democratize the semidemocratic Legislative Council.

The central government in Beijing should realize Hong Kong's political system is unsustainable and must be fixed to make it more responsive to people in the territory. Each of the Chief Executives handpicked by Beijing has proven deeply unpopular with significant numbers of people in Hong Kong. At the political level, it would be encouraging if the senior leadership in Beijing could accept the idea that people in the mainland and Hong Kong want democracy, and not construe Hong Kong peoples' demands for democracy as a threat to national security. At a minimum, Beijing should stop arresting people in the mainland for peaceful expressions of support to the demonstrators, and lift whatever restrictions have been put in place so that demonstrators can enter the mainland.

It is encouraging to see the reestablishment of a Hong Kong caucus here in the Congress, and the introduction of an updated Hong Kong Policy Act. We believe that increased U.S. Government scrutiny and regular reporting are and should be seen as a positive obligation—an opportunity to identify critical developments and points of leverage in a territory of considerable diplomatic, economic, and strategic interest to the United States. Equally important, we urge the U.S. to be consistent in its support to democratic movements around the world. The people of Hong Kong deserve no less than their counterparts in other countries.

Senator CARDIN. So, I want to start, Dr. Bush, if I might, with your expertise in Taiwan. The reports that I have read indicate that what happened in Hong Kong had a direct impact on election results in Taiwan. So, I guess my point is, Secretary Russel said that we are watching, is the international community in the region watching what is happening in Hong Kong? And what impact does it have on the region itself?

Dr. BUSH. Thanks for the question.

Let me endorse your general point. And that is, what China does in Hong Kong is going to give us an important signal of what kind of great power it is going to be. If this can somehow work out well, that would suggest a China that maybe we can live with. If it works out badly, that is a very different and negative message.

With respect to Taiwan, frankly, there were a lot of issues at play, and we do not have the polling results yet to know how much Hong Kong made a difference. Obviously, it made some. I would say that people on Taiwan have long since dissociated themselves from the Hong Kong arrangements. They have always believed that they do not apply to them. So, when things go badly in Hong Kong, the attitude is, ''Well, this just proves it.'' But, I think, you know, among certain groups, it did have an impact. I think the results of the election, which were very much antiestablishment, also had an effect on Hong Kong in building up a certain level of enthusiasm this last weekend.

Senator CARDIN. Thank you.

Dr. Richardson, I want to get your view on the human rights status in Hong Kong. In 1992, we said human rights are of great importance to the United States and directly relevant to U.S. interests in Hong Kong. Hong Kong enjoys a distinct status with the United States, even though it is ''one country, two systems.'' And our relationship with China is remarkably different than it is with Hong Kong, as I am sure you are aware.

Most recently, the violence against protesters and the inability of British parliamentarians to be able to visit and see firsthand whether they are in compliance with their agreements—of great concern to us. Can you just give me your assessment as to the current status of basic human rights in Hong Kong?

Dr. RICHARDSON. Thank you very much for the question.

You know, Hong Kong has historically been the bastion of rights in this part of the world. And I think part of the reason we are having this conversation today is because it is the democratic part of China. Obviously, there is room for greater growth for political rights, but I think, as the bulwark that we want protect, it is critically important.

We have been very concerned, over the last year or two, about growing threats to Hong Kong's autonomy, but also—and, as a related matter, limitations on issues ranging from press freedom to immigration to certain court decisions about who has access to which kinds of government services. In the past year in particular, we have tracked what appear to be growing problems with respect to surveillance, particularly of either mainland activists or ethnic

Chinese activists from other parts of the world who are in Hong Kong for obvious reasons, to have some contact with counterparts.

I think the protests have been a little bit mischaracterized as simply being either carried out by students or specifically about the particularities of the nomination process or electoral arrangements. I think there is a much broader statement being made by a cross-section of people in Hong Kong who are increasingly concerned about their own ability to affect or command the attention of the Hong Kong Government. And I think, obviously, the nomination process is enormously problematic from a human rights perspective. I mean, this is black-letter international law, that people should have the right to run. You know, so this gives you a sense of some of the kinds of problems that Hong Kong's status is the place of a free press, that is safe for activists to operate, and where people can expect police to refrain from use of excessive force, which obviously has been an issue of real concern over the last 6 weeks, you know, where those problems do not pertain.

Senator CARDIN. Hong Kong enjoys——

Dr. BUSH. Could I just comment for——

Senator CARDIN. Yes.

Dr. BUSH. I am sorry.

I think the danger in the current situation is that if some sensible compromise is not worked out along the lines of what Secretary Russel was talking about—and I think there is still a chance—that protests will continue and China will ratchet up or place greater limits on the human rights of people in Hong Kong, and particularly political rights. And this will not be obvious, this will not be out in the open. It will be somewhat covert, but it will have an impact.

Senator CARDIN. Hong Kong's special status in economic power in large part depends on an open relationship with the United States. What recommendations would you make as to how we leverage that relationship in order to advance basic rights in Hong Kong? And, if you want to, you can comment about the legislation that has been filed that would change the presumption. It would require the President to certify that Hong Kong is in status in order to be able to get the status, rather than currently, which requires the President to take affirmative action to deny them the special status. Your comments on how you would like to see the United States use its leverage with Hong Kong—or use its relationship with Hong Kong to leverage greater respect for democratic principles, human rights, and universal suffrage.

Dr. RICHARDSON. I think there are a couple of broad areas to focus on. The first is about linkage and leverage. I think there is less of an effort now than there was 10 years ago to link specific changes to specific policy initiatives, for example. I think the Chinese Government is extremely transactional on these kinds of matters, and it is essential for the United States to use what Beijing wants as a way to press for what the United States wants. And so, for example, the Chinese Government is seeking much greater United States cooperation on terrorism and counter-terrorism issues, about which we have some real concerns. Separate matter. But, I see no reason, you know, why the United States should not, or could not, say that revising the electoral arrangements in Hong Kong, per article 45 of the Basic Law, is a requirement for further cooperation in some of those other realms. I think there are a lot of opportunities for linkage that are not being pursued.

I respectfully disagree with Assistant Secretary Russel about the U.S. Government's rhetoric when it has mostly, I think, been factually accurate. I think it has been muted. It has not necessarily been deployed when it was needed most. And I think, to a large extent, it has not really reached the people in Hong Kong who needed or wanted to hear it. I think the United States continues to be quite inconsistent about issues about political rights and democracy in Hong Kong and China, relative to the kind of support that it chose for those issues in other parts of the world. And being consistent, I think, matters enormously with Beijing.

Senator CARDIN. Dr. Bush.

Dr. BUSH. Thank you very much.

If there is a possibility, along the lines of what Secretary Russel was saying, of getting a competitive election out of this current unfortunate situation, then we should be working with all sides in Hong Kong, both the Hong Kong government and people in the pan-democratic camp to help, perhaps behind the scenes, to bring it about. But, the important thing is that we are effective.

With respect to the legislation that you have introduced, I fully support restoring a periodic report by the Department of State concerning developments in Hong Kong and how they relate to the standards set forth in the act.

I am agnostic on the issue of certification. I guess my main concern has to do with the definitions of what one is going to be certifying—laws, agreements, and arrangements. It is not clear what "arrangements" are. It could be some very specific things, it could be very general. And so, I would encourage some work on defining what it is that is going to be certified. I do believe that the autonomy is very important. I worked on the House Foreign Affairs Committee, and I was the lead staffer on the House side in 1992 on the United States-Hong Kong Policy Act. And, for me, section 201 about Hong Kong's autonomy was absolutely the most important section. It remains the important section. I think that it should be possible, between this committee and the administration, to work out an effective way to ensure that that autonomy is preserved.

Senator CARDIN. That is—yes, Dr.——

Dr. RICHARDSON. Sorry, may I follow up, quickly?

We are proponents of the idea of reinstating the reporting, in no small part because—look, even if the issue about the nomination committee gets resolved—and I am skeptical about the Hong Kong government's willingness and ability to accurately represent the views of people in Hong Kong to the Central Government and push for a better outcome—but, this is not the end of the line. It is very clear, I think, that the Chinese Government intends to find ways to try to manipulate membership of Ledgco, of what its agenda could possibly include. We are going to be fighting this battle for a long time, and I think having those kind of reports in hand can be a very useful tool.

Senator CARDIN. This is a good transition to the principal Republican sponsor of the legislation, Senator Rubio. [Laughter.]

Senator RUBIO. Thank you. And I know we have votes, so I will be quick. I have two questions; one for you, Dr. Richardson.

I look at the U.S. response to this, and it seems like the majority of our statements are designed to prove that we have nothing to do with what is going on, as opposed to standing on behalf of the people that are fighting. In fact, you saw that in the testimony today, that the rationale behind the statement was, we wanted to make clear that we were not behind any one group versus another. And that should be 10 percent of what we talk about. Ninety percent of this should be about democracy. Can you contrast what the U.S. reaction has been to what is happening in Hong Kong to the position the United States has taken in other parts of the world where there has been democracy movements, whether it is Burma or Ukraine or other parts of the world? How would you compare the U.S. reaction to this versus the U.S. reaction to other democracy movements around the world?

Dr. RICHARDSON. Well, I think you can look at it in a couple of different ways. You know, I find myself thinking about, for example, Assistant Secretary Nuland walking out into Maidan Square and handing bread to people. You know, it was a very evocative response, a gesture of support. You know, obviously, there are different circumstances, but, you know, clearly the United States is capable of very demonstrably showing its support in certain circumstances.

Look at, you know, what the President said when he was in Beijing. Again, you know, factually accurate in making the right points, but, I think, in a way that was maximally designed not to irk his hosts. I do not mean to belittle the blowback that Assistant Secretary Russel will have received for that. But, you can see that it is so calibrated as to become convoluted. Fast-forward 36 hours, when the President is in Burma, where he is speaking very clearly, very evocatively, and in great detail about the importance of democracy, elections, the particulars of the electoral arrangements. I think that really sends a message to pro-democracy activists in Hong Kong and in the mainland that they should not have, necessarily, terribly high hopes for the kind of support that they are going to get from the United States in these circumstances.

Senator RUBIO. I think the bottom line is that it is clear that our response to the democratic aspirations of people on the mainland or anywhere else when it comes to China are muted by real realpolitik considerations with regarding to China's influence and size. In essence, if you want democracy—if you are going to fight for democracy and democratic openings in a place where China does not want it, you are not going to get the same response from the United States that you would in other parts of the world, because we do not want to ruin our relationship with the Chinese. That is the message that people are taking. And I think it is a counterproductive one.

And then, my question for you, Dr. Bush, is, If you put yourself in the position now of people in Taiwan—or, for that matter, any other nation in East Asia—as they look at Hong Kong as indicative of the nature of the Chinese Government, what are they taking away from what they are seeing right now?

Dr. BUSH. If you were a citizen of a country in Asia, and if you had watched what has happened in Hong Kong over the last 20-plus years, you would understand pretty clearly that the Chinese Government rigged this political system to keep its friends in power. And that system is illegitimate. The leaders who are produced by it do not have the support of the people. Hong Kong is now unstable because of that. So, if you want stability in Hong Kong, which China says it does, if you want stability anywhere, it needs to be based on an open, competitive, democratic system. That is the way to get legitimate governments.

Senator RUBIO. But, that is not what they offer.

Dr. BUSH. No, it is not. There are ways, I think, of working, even within the narrow confines to facilitate a competitive election. I am not terribly optimistic that it is going to work out that way. But, if they go in the direction that you fear and that I fear, they will continue to face problems in Hong Kong.

Senator RUBIO. So, my understanding is that the Chinese proposal for what it wants to see Taiwan become is very similar to the Hong Kong model.

Dr. BUSH. The slogan is the same, and it has been rejected by Taiwan people——

Senator RUBIO. They know better.

Dr. BUSH. They know much better. For all its problems, Taiwan people like the democracy that they have, and they do not want to go backward, which is where they see Hong Kong is in relation to them.

Senator RUBIO. Is it fair to say—and this is my last question—that looking at what is happening in Hong Kong now is a true indication of the nature of the Central Government, and that, moving forward, all of us who care about future of China's rise in the world, but also its relationship with the United States and with its neighbors, needs to realize that what they say—you know, they go into these international forums, they smile, and they say one thing, and what they are going to do—are two very different things. When they talk about autonomy, when they talk about democratic opening, what it means to them is very different from what we think it means. And so, that is where you wind up in a situation like what we have today, where we have someone testifying on behalf of the State Department and the administration that the agreement does not violate the letter of the agreement, but it violates the spirit of it. In essence, they may use the same terms that we use, but, in practice, they are not the same terms. And the lesson to be learned is, that is the true nature of this government, for anyone who is looking to do a future arrangement or agreement with them.

Dr. BUSH. Anybody who has studied China professionally knows that their definition of terms is not our definition of terms. And we have to adjust our diplomacy to take account of that. I think Hong Kong people understand that China's use of terms is not their use of terms, either.

Thanks.

Senator CARDIN. Let me thank both of our witnesses.

I think there is agreement here that, where we normally look for pragmatism to deal with diplomatic issues, in this situation it does not work, because the consequences are far beyond what is happening Hong Kong today. As Senator Rubio pointed out, and as Dr. Bush pointed out earlier to my question, the impact on Taiwan is very clear, the impact on a lot of Asian countries is very clear, because of their relationships with China and China's importance in the region and whether they will adhere to understandings that are pretty clear. And, in Hong Kong, it was very clear that Hong Kong would be autonomous, as Secretary Russel said—''one country, two systems,'' but it would have the autonomy. You do not have the autonomy unless you have the right to select your leader. And that was clear in the initial declaration, original commitments to have universal suffrage, which clearly the August declaration statement backed away from. I could not agree more with Senator Rubio that this is not a technical violation, et cetera, that this is clearly inconsistent and totally against the commitment made by China for allowing universal suffrage. And it is a matter that we need to be very clear about. And I think you will hear clear statements on this subject from the Members of the Senate.

We have potential action. Senator Rubio has a bill that he has filed, and I know that it will be on our agenda next year. And we certainly will be watching this issue very carefully. We will see how they are dealing with basic human rights, including how they deal with the demonstrators and how they deal with allowing people access, something you would normally expect from an open society that Hong Kong claims it is. That will be matters that will be very carefully watched, not just by the Members of the U.S. Senate, but I think by the global community.

So, I want to thank both of you for your contributions to this hearing and your understanding of how we had to abbreviate it to deal with the realities of the Senate schedule.

And, with that, the subcommittee will stand adjourned.

[Whereupon, at 10:17 a.m., the hearing was adjourned.]

ADDITIONAL MATERIAL SUBMITTED FOR THE RECORD

SUBMITTED WRITTEN TESTIMONY OF ELLEN BORK, SENIOR FELLOW, FOREIGN POLICY INITIATIVE

I am grateful to Chairman Rubio and members of the subcommittee for this opportunity to submit testimony for the record of this important hearing.

The protesters who began occupying Hong Kong's streets in late September have not achieved their objective: the democratic election of the Chief Executive who runs the affairs of Hong Kong's 7.2 million people. Neither the Hong Kong government, nor the central government in Beijing has shown any flexibility regarding an August 31 ruling of the National People's Congress Standing Committee in Beijing that in future Hong Kong voters will choose their chief executive from among candidates approved by Beijing with the additional criterion that they must ''love the Country and love Hong Kong,'' or, in other words, be loyal to the Chinese Communist Party.

Instead, the Chinese Government has dubbed the protests illegal and the Hong Kong authorities acting on Beijing's behalf refuse to countenance any change from the Basic Law, Beijing's ''constitution'' for Hong Kong. As of this writing, some protest leaders are on a hunger strike. Others have turned themselves in to the police as a further gesture of civil disobedience. The police and court officials are whittling down protest encampments and the student group at the forefront of the protests has suggested it may call for an end to street demonstrations.

Whatever happens next, there is no returning to the status quo ante for the people of Hong Kong, for China's Communist leadership, or for the United States. Chinese leaders have demonstrated decisively that they do not intend to allow Hong Kong autonomy or a transition to democratic government, regardless of any commitments they may have made in the past. Hong Kong's democracy movement has been reinvigorated by a surge of participation by the youngest citizens. Meanwhile, all of Hong Kong is developing an identity, distinct from the mainland, linked to Hong Kong's rule of law, civil liberties and in reaction against Beijing's obstruction of democracy. In response to these developments, U.S. policy devised to fit the circumstances at the time of the 1997 handover of Hong Kong to Chinese rule, needs to be revised.

As Members of Congress think about how to do that, I respectfully suggest they keep several points in mind.

A new generation of younger and student activists has transformed Hong Kong's democracy movement. Recent surveys show strong support for democracy among the population at large and especially among youth and young adults. Student protest leaders have eclipsed the older, established pro-democracy politicians whom they regard, even if unfairly, as tainted by participation in the post-1997 institutions set up by Beijing to contain, rather than advance democracy, such as the only partly elected Legislative Council. Aware of this, the leadership of the pro-democracy political parties exhibited a striking degree of deference to the student leaders.

At the same time, Hong Kong is developing a distinct identity. The number of people who identify themselves as "Chinese" or with reference to the PRC has fallen according to the Hong Kong University Public Opinion Program which asks Hong Kong people about their ethnic identity, offering a number of categories which reflect their attachment to a Hong Kong, Chinese, or other identities. According to the survey, "Both the indices of "Chinese" and "citizens of the PRC" are once again at their lowest since the compilation of these indices in 2008. . . . The feeling of being "citizens of the PRC" is the weakest among all identities tested." These sentiments were on display at the Umbrella movement protests. "I wouldn't say I reject my identity as Chinese, because I've never felt Chinese in the first place," one protester told Edward Wong of the New York Times. "The younger generations don't think they're Chinese."

It's useful to remember that the "one country, two systems" concept has its origins in Beijing's desire to entice Taiwan to unify with Communist China in the late 1970s. Since then, Taiwan has democratized, and with it, developed a strong Taiwanese identity, making it ever more unlikely that Taiwan will agree to come under Communist Chinese rule absent coercion. Unlike Hong Kong, Taiwan has a defense commitment from the U.S. and American policy now includes a stipulation that any resolution of Taiwan's fate must be acceptable to people on both sides of the Strait.

By contrast, Hong Kong people had no say in whether they were to be handed over to Communist rule. Many in the younger generation look askance at the system and institutions Beijing created for post-1997 Hong Kong. The arrangements between China and Great Britain were made in early 1980s, before many of the current protesters were born, and over the heads of their parents.

The failure of China's plans to deliver democracy and guarantee autonomy was predictable. "To a Westerner," the historian Steve Tsang wrote in 1996, "the idea of Hong Kong people administering Hong Kong within the framework of 'one country, two systems' may imply that after 1997 Hong Kong will be free to run its own domestic affairs with no interference from Beijing as long as PRC sovereignty is acknowledged. Such an interpretation is totally unacceptable to Beijing."

The Umbrella movement has made it impossible to pretend any longer that Beijing intends to allow Hong Kong autonomy and democracy. Yet so far, despite support for Hong Kong's autonomy and democracy in the U.S.-Hong Kong Policy Act, the Obama administration has made it clear that will not confront Beijing over its actions, or seriously support democracy in Hong Kong.

In late September, just as the protests were breaking out, the U.S. consulate in Hong Kong stated that America "does not take sides" regarding Hong Kong's democracy struggle. Little had changed by November 12, when President Obama spoke about Hong Kong in Beijing during a joint press conference with General Secretary Xi Jinping. President Obama appeared to be primarily concerned with assuring Mr. Xi that the U.S. was not interfering in Hong Kong affairs. The President acquiesced to the end of the protests—without any concessions by the Chinese Government toward democracy—so long as no violence was used. President Obama did not mention Beijing's detention of dozens of people on the mainland for brave actions endorsing the Hong Kong democracy movement, or the massive censorship of Hong Kong related content on the Chinese Internet.

"Ultimately," President Obama said, the issues underlying the protests; i.e., democracy and elections, were "for the people of Hong Kong and the people of China to decide." This depiction of the democracy struggle in Hong Kong and China as taking place on an even playing field was problematic to say the least. By presenting the U.S. as a disinterested bystander, the President delivered a setback not only to the Hong Kong protesters but also to those working for democracy in the rest of China, in Russia and Iran and other places and gave a boost to the dictatorships in those and other countries.

The premises on which U.S. policy and law are based are no longer valid. The thrust of current law is that Washington will respond to violations of Hong Kong's autonomy by withdrawing Hong Kong's separate treatment in some areas of U.S. law. That punishes the victim rather than the perpetrator. Instead, the U.S. should look for ways to impose costs on the central government and officials responsible for Hong Kong affairs. Chinese officials (and their relatives) who make or stash money in Hong Kong even while undermining Hong Kong's democratic aspirations are an appropriate target for financial or visa sanctions. Congress might ask to be briefed by the executive branch about the assets and travels of such officials.

''One country, two systems'' is not working—at least not the version that Hong Kong people were led to believe in. Recent events show that whether democracy advances in Hong Kong depends on principle and power, not China's fake constitutionalism and not even of international obligations China undertook in the Sino-British Joint Declaration.

It has become commonplace to remark that the Umbrella Movement has changed Hong Kong forever. It is not yet clear whether the U.S. policy will also respond to this momentous change.